Air Tea With
Dolores

D1558772

Critical Praise for the books of Djelloul Marbrook

Artemisia's Wolf (title story, *A Warding Circle*)

. . . successfully blends humor and satire (and perhaps even a touch of magic realism) into its short length . . . an engrossing story, but what might strike the reader most throughout the book is its infusion of breathtaking poetry. . . a stunning rebuke to notoriously misogynist subcultures like the New York art scene, showing us just how hard it is for a young woman to be judged on her creative talent alone.

—Tommy Zurhellen, *Hudson River Valley Review*

Saraceno

. . . Djelloul Marbrook writes dialogue that not only entertains with an intoxicating clickety-clack, but also packs a truth about low-life mob culture *The Sopranos* only hints at. You can practically smell the anisette and filling-station coffee.

—Dan Baum, author of *Gun Guys* (2013), *Nine Lives: Mystery, Magic, Death and Life in New Orleans* (2009) and others

. . . a good ear for crackling dialogue . . . I love Marbrook's crude, raw music of the streets. The notes are authentic and on target . . .

—Sam Coale, *The Providence (RI) Journal*

. . . an entirely new variety of gangster tale . . . a Mafia story sculpted with the most refined of sensibilities from the clay of high art and philosophy . . . the kind of writer I take real pleasure in discovering . . . a mature artist whose rich body of work is finally coming to light.

—Brent Robison, editor, *Prima Materia*

Far from Algiers

. . . as succinct as most stanzas by Dickinson. . . an unusually mature, confidently composed first poetry collection.

—Susanna Roxman, *Prairie Schooner*

. . . brings together the energy of a young poet with the wisdom of long experience.

—Edward Hirsch, Guggenheim Foundation

Brushstrokes and Glances

Whether it is commentary on state power, corporate greed, or the intensely personal death of a loved one, Djelloul Marbrook is clear-sighted, eloquent, and precise. As the title of the collection suggests, he uses the lightest touch, a collection of fragments, brushstrokes and glances, to fashion poems that resonate with truth and honesty.

—Phil Constable, *New York Journal of Books*

Air Tea With Dolores

poems by

Djelloul Marbrook

LEAKY BOOT PRESS

Air Tea With Dolores
by Djelloul Marbrook

Acknowledgments

"Air tea with Dolores" was published in the fall 2011
issue of *Northport Literary Journal.*
"I worked in a taxidermy studio" was published in
The Ledge Poetry and Fiction Magazine, Winter 2009-10,
and in *The Country and Abroad,* June 2008.

First published in 2017 by
Leaky Boot Press
http://www.leakyboot.com

ISBN: 978-1-909849-26-6

Six years old. I felt horror at the stony order of the world.
—Czeslaw Milosz
from "Treatise on Theology" in *Second Space,* 2004

Contents

YOU SAW NOTHING?

CRYSTAL SHIP

BLOOD AND ALL THAT

TREE OF LIES

CODA

Proem

Carrots still to pull

Concord grapes and dew,
carrots still to pull,
Daisy and Dolly nuzzling
a boy at his homework
in a frozen barn—
that's the innocence
waking an old man up
with such fragrances,
such exuberances
he might have thought
he had another life to live
had it not been for the pain
of not remembering a day
when he felt safe in bed.

Rubies and trust

Where are you now?

Will you love me forever & ever,
cross your heart and hope to die?
He took the hope-to-die part seriously
& to do that he had to cross his heart
again & again, not knowing once you do
it becomes your unbecoming.
You were capable of love,
having no idea what it was
or what was to come—
the future was a bother,
the past a sore. You gladly fell
into the well of her eyes
and never climbed out,
& when she left you found
she had taken you with her.

That first kiss

Of some teachers and errant gods
I would have to say they drink
of children's fragrances too much
and dream of them as voodoo dolls.

But I don't have to say it, do I,
or do I say it because it's well
to remember the flagrant spell
of godlings who knew what to do?

Flash of leg and eye, what to skirt?
What not to mention when I knew
my perfume was of such importance
it pulled their mouths askew?

It's as hard to be honest about this
as it is to believe in faeries
and yet the taste is as memorable
as that first apocalyptic kiss.

Not even gods in all that budding
and petaled innocence survive,
at least not as they found it.
I know I did not get out alive.

Dolores

Abhorrence of fingernails, wariness of teeth—
I will honor a people who honor molested girls
and spend their time considering
why boys grow up to kill each other.

She stared at fingers and studied teeth,
and I wake in the middle of my old age
dizzy with her scent. I hope she isn't listening
to a clock in a nursing home, I hope snow

is dusting her great blue coat as she minds
sleeping, burlapped roses in an English garden
and I hope she knows I can't imagine dying
not having learned to swim in her eyes.

Troublesome daughter

Her safety whistle deafened daddy,
left him no good for anything,
that is, better than he was before.

Her laser eye closed the wound
her mother called a marriage,
and the door to any kind of home,

and so for her vestigial gifts
she was homeless in the midst
of a professing family, itching

in their glamored wool.
She became a marginal note
for having seen and read so well.

Amusement park

In the house of horrors I'm okay,
My cardboard suitcase and rag bunny
shall fear no evil even if I fail
to reach Gomorrah. Satan
will serve the usual dirty-water dogs
in the park and I will be arrested

for indecent exposure of things
I left unsaid in the attic when
Dolores and I decided the rest of it
was not for us and we would stay
there after the others grew up
and always be better than friends

and more than that other they
talked about as if growing up
was something we could do
in our spare time and old age
a place where cowards scramble
after swimming Hell Gate in winter.

Air tea with Dolores

When I think of *dying to* I think of air tea with Dolores,
    air tea in painted tin cups in a crumbling gazebo—

whatever was more privileged than air tea with Dolores?
    I have never been dying to have more than that.

For all my deadly curiosity, I never wanted to know
    anyone more than Dolores, never wanted to know

anything about anyone more than the number of hairs
    on her thighs or her dizzying breath.

Many of us die to know important people; after Dolores
    I saw only people putting on airs. Air tea

with Dolores corrected the courses of shooting stars
    but could not protect us from our predators:

after I was raped and nearly hung I decided to be a beam
    in the novas of her eyes, and I believed

we were separated because I no longer deserved
    air tea with Dolores, the tipsiness of her breath,

no longer deserved anything, anyone, and no more would be able
    to die to know even one profane secret.

I know more about heaven than I should because I know
    it won't be as lovely as air tea with Dolores.

Rubies and trust

Assuming we need God more than we need enemies,
I'd like to propose a loony's heresy, that each mind
is the microcosm of the cosmos. Free of the tyranny
of the anthromorph, opinion would be a broken tool
and we would flash and orbit in each other's eyes
just as we faint and marvel in the grandeur of night skies.

From that privet chapel where I prayed to be yew
to this crackling decrepitude of stars and splendor
I stumbled and crashed through desire's bullbriar
to arrive a blinding combustion of rubies and trust
that I see the cosmos wherever there is sentience
and have no need to redesign or quibble with a dot.

I worked in a taxidermy studio

I know how a leopard's hide feels,
harder than tigers, softer than bears.
I have broken three-sided needles
on a polar bear's knee and dozed
among jaguars and Angora goats.
No one will stretch me on a manikin
or line me with felt and twill,
give me glass eyes and a waxen tongue,
but if I could comfort children,
that would be a worthy ambition.
More likely some photographer
would recruit me for a Revlon ad
and I'd be classier than I've ever been
and forget about the little boy
who repaired the hunter's wound
and imagined my pounding heart.

Glint

Keep this glint safe for me,
I will not ask it back.
I have been watching you
as if it were a dream
from which I can't wake
and trust you more
than this unfamiliar self.

We don't know for whom we wait,
we're not what we deserve,
but the perfect moment comes to hand.

You don't even need to know
if I'm a pebble or a daisy,
just take care of me. We'll meet
in a stream bed under water
as night cinders or fireflies.

Trust me, trust me not, I'll come again
and you'll be there, a little girl
cupping something in your hands
your life depends on showing me.

Destroys his mother's life

The 25th hour

I chose the 25th hour to be born
to frustrate astrologers
and elude my parents' ken.
If I had to forget my friends
or even that I'd come from somewhere
for the privilege of this roller-coaster ride
I thought there should be something fey
about my data or around my eyes—
a whim for which the cost has been usurious.
Yeah, yeah, I know, compared to what?
I can tell you first thing in the morning
before things get too bright and big,
too loud, too entirely mundane,
but when I brush my teeth I forget
because then I'm ready to eat
and pretend to be awake.
I chose the 25th hour to be born
to keep the door open behind me,
to keep hot air from blowing it shut.

Store windows

At age two I destroyed my mother's life,
then I spent the rest of mine counting what I miss,
a project as old as Gilgamesh.

Life has been one long old home week
going back there wherever there is
and trying to figure out how I acquired all that power.

Just lucky, I guess. Now as for what I miss,
that's what I need mathematics for, and even then
I can't see how it can all go on without me.

I stare in windows to make sure I'm still there,
creaky old me and teen-age girls, we know
what happens when you turn around too fast

and notice nobody's there, not even you.
No, it's not our vanity, it's our certain knowledge
that nothing we've ever been told can be trusted.

Nothing, not even our names, and as for our looks,
to whom do they really belong? That's why we need
store windows and sidelong glances.

This dangerous boy

The little boy who couldn't blink,
his secret eye stuck open,
would never be easy to love.

No one wants to be that naked,
though it's not nakedness he sees
but the ancients in our faces,

ancients and societies howling
because given their chance again
they do no better than before.

Privet chapel

Stars electric swarm
a privet chapel where
a boy prays for wings to leave
leaden bloodiness here.

If all those guardians could ignore
bloody sheets and clothes,
gasp and wheeze and disappearance
of a smile replaced by a sob
that in a child is euphemism
for the implosion of a star,
then to grow up is to clean up
evidence of the cruelest crimes.

Religion forbidden here,
miracles and savaged children
only are allowed. Wonder,
stigmata and wings
accepted conditions. Words
suspect but permitted
in emergencies such as these.

Dolly and Daisy

Dolly and Daisy wore fedoras in winter,
Panamas in summer,
and wouldn't leave the barn without them
because an oddity without respect
won't plow straight or stand still
for children to reach the highest grapes.
Dolly and Daisy expected me
to ward off lightning and sing
of bluebirds over the white cliffs of Dover
which none of us would ever see.

Peggy's love

How did that beaming boy
in the wicker stroller
on a Brooklyn street
come by this face
whose consequences
shock me over counters
and in crowded rooms?

His nanny's one true love
by Peggy's own account
now pokes moray eels
dozing in cashiers' minds.
Not a face men wish well,
a face reminding women
of grievance and mistake.

What Peggy Connors saw
is pentimento now:
grief and betrayal scrape
innocent flesh away
and bone awakes
resentments lulled
to precarious sleep.

Hysteria

Raise your hand if hideous laughter
is your ecstatic spurt
across the yawing womb of misery.
Shame's irrelevant. Raise your hand,
paint your madness on the ceiling.
You know how primates ape
the looniest of their number
and suicide weaves a daisy chain
to crown the skull beneath.
When this laughter is a wilding in my throat
I think tears the proper ink of history
and blood is bathos and opera.
I came to this bacchanal
uncertain of my innocence
and was perceived
an otherling whose osprey stare
and nictating eye discomfited.
To partake or be partaken—
I didn't know and so emit
this laugh only when I stumble
on remnants of the orgy.
Raise your hand if you feared
to giggle at a funeral or object
at a wedding, if you prefer
chaos to membership and people
drift through the hole in your heart.

If the Norsemen
haven't come

Sudden . . .

(Incident at boarding school)

Squealing kids are lynching me again
with the best of intentions of course.

I smile and wriggle in my skin
wanting to be like them, longing

to swat those buzzing bloody bugs.
My body enjoys a second's elongation.

What has changed? Daisy and Dolly neigh
and stomp. My feet climb the air,

and then I remember (it becomes a habit)
my hands are free and I begin to climb

hand over hand up the murder rope
giving a neighbor time to cut me down.

I almost share their disappointment
watching me scamper along the hoist.

Every time an innocent monster squeals
my bulging eyes fill with the shadowless bay,

my skin comes off, my heart turns around.
I came here to be hung, my escape

is a deviation from the plan and after it
I am on my own again and again

whenever a child squeals with joy
or complaint, joy my hands are pulling

at the noose, complaint I'm climbing up
out of my predicament. Here to be hung

but occasionally forgetting it until
a child shrieks, a mother looks away.

I remember the horses, how I'll miss them,
but I won't miss the shadowless bay.

I'll even miss you if you forget to tie my hands.
Malarial this stress disorder helping

everyone to make strange, turning
familiar places to new prisons, disordering

my senses till they shout with anger.
Everyone comes up behind me,

whatever happens is a shock,
my permanent state is dismay.

Home is where I don't have to climb a rope,
but will I remember that when I get there?

The scent of trespass

Roads rake revenant earth,
wildflowers deify the scabs;
this would be enough
to reify me if my wounds
did not bloom at night,
dizzy me with red chaos
and the fragrance of grief.

From great distances I smell
those who trespassed me;
it's good for them their lovers
don't have my rabbit's nose.
Their scents could be sold
in vials for obscene prices.
I follow them in dreams

to gangs of women ululating
but not for me, balconies
clamoring with desire
but not for halflings fading
across the street and leaving
only a pair of inhuman eyes.
Night trains ululate for me.

Introspection and panic

Why blades of light should prise
the reassuring dark of native 4 a.m.
in my dreams confounded me until
I tracked them to a blazing plotting room
where my guardians covered up a crime,
ordering someone to burn my sheets.

Even if they had turned out the lights
hands of light would part the filmy years
to slide back these stage sets
revealing my life as sly theater.
To know what cannot be repaired
is melancholy grace beyond compare.

Great South Bay

His spirit deserts a child

You lost your heart for the slog.
Did you foresee it unfold?
You chose to die back there
in a privet chapel where we prayed
to ward the U-boats off Great South Bay.
I think that when I left you
to weed my Chinese cabbage I knew
you'd be gone when I came back.
I kept on talking as if you were there,
I knew you'd quit and taken my name,
and because there was no more you
it didn't matter what anyone called me.
It was you who needed the name.
Your decision darkens me:
you should have lived this life,
you were the strong invisible one,
you would have known what to do.
You left me to a world that revolted you.
How could I prosper in it?
No one would have expected my wound to heal
—chin up, soldier on, and all that crap—
but who expected you to fall down?
I would have carried you all this way.
Instead I have your desertion to bear.
You understood the wounds were grave,
I knew just enough to be a revenant.

If I had to guess at your despair
after these sixty and more years I'd say
it was because you couldn't make me weep.
I know you tried, I know you left a sob
in my chest that never dissolved in the tumult
of ordinary life, a sob to remember you by,
a sob and my failure to cry.
Whoever corrupts a child deafens him to angels
and sets him down among demons.

Her crime still thrills an old woman

Thoughts infecting me act on their own,
I celebrate the disease. He was seven
when my robe fell open. No one else
will ever own him. This is all I know at root:
Aisling Wynant, my name then, is his soil.
He was mine, he smelled me, and I spanked him
for some cooked-up offense. His real offense
was seeing me without intent, with eyes
that didn't belong in anyone's head and were bound
to get him in trouble in my lap and everywhere
corrupters sweat in the presence of children
who've accidentally landed here.
I picked him out because I could, being resident god,
and that singular honor bewitched him,
as it would, so he came to chapel often
to worship face down at my altar.
I gave him sacred privileges but couldn't keep
him to myself. Others craved and ruined him.
I've never told lovers a boy is watching us,
touching in me what no one else can find.
I bet my taste will haunt his ashes. Is he gone?
I would know; there would be a numbness.
We were awake. Can the moral say as much?
The school is now a fundamentalist church—
do you think baking soda rids them of our scent?

44

I'd repent if I hadn't been his luck. I hope
he knows some of us are visitors, not subject
to the ways you bore yourselves to death,
subject to what we get away with and only
if it illumines something in the night.

The rapist

Certain knotted calves cast evenings
where I'd like to live. On certain ankles
hopeless beauties topple. I like to catch the petals
but I don't care to press them in a book.
Eyes are overrated, reminding of the sea.
What hands express at rest
tells you all you need to know
if you follow close and slow,
if you're not distracted by antic things.
Hands will tell you if repose
resides anywhere close to use.
Wrists are more forensic than toes.
You wouldn't think I'd know.
My name is Christian Killian:
you need a soul to be distracted
by datum and determinant.
I was rid of it when I raped him
and never looked at him again.
I chose to choreograph women
that in their compliance and sweat
I might forget how he stared at me.
Now I'm happily unburdened, free
to contemplate the hand,
the one I had in ruining him.
My image fights its forming in a glass,
my portraitist has noted this.
There are equanimities that smack
of too much practice, mine pirates light
because it has none of its own.

45

Have you noticed this? The peculiar shine
of actors? Isn't it what we worship
nowadays? I fit right well, I travel light
without the soul I left in that damned boy's cot.
It seems a thousand years ago
in an America now so chic to revile.
He loved baseball. My wife rides horses.
I hate her shining face
that takes the dark I reek for gravitas.
I hate their faces that take me for a gentleman
because I never did such a thing again.
There are days when I'd consider it success
if my image gurgled down the sink
and I never came downstairs
uttering banalities that itch my teeth.
At night my scalp crawls off my head
revealing nests of vipers twined
around my hatred of two lost boys.
I smell bad in silks, I know what power is.

The boy's spirit looks back

You don't remember green clouds lowering,
lightning piping me to heaven in a squall.
I could see through red blindfolds
and not be made to turn away.
Your friends wept in their pillows for English homes.
They'd come to escape the Luftwaffe, but you
sent me home from the horrors of that camp.
Gods can save anyone but themselves
and that is why they have their stories.
Now your story's somewhat different.
You thought you called up that hell
by some ill omen in you and you saw
no reason I should suffer it—
how is it now you speak of my deserting,
speaking too cogently to be believed?

Why should the bastards have gotten two for one?
Your decent act hardened to a lie.
I took your name because a revenant
has no more need of it than clothes.
I was a young goblin—you said an angel—
I never thought I'd be watching you
with as much love as you had for me,
and once I knew it was my lot, how
could I have known it would be so hard?
I'm as brave a watcher as you're a fool—
you can't always win at craps or fake a life.
If you're lame you limp, if mutilated
you can only pretend. You suffered cruelty:
people who couldn't be bothered called it the breaks—
so let's call those breaks beyond repair.
You're beyond repair, what's left of you.
That has been your condition for a long time.
You tried to steal home on one leg
and the ghouls in the stands encouraged you.
You exiled your witness and called it growing up.
Stuck in a pool of blood, you couldn't prove the crimes.
What am I going to do with you
now your song is almost sung?

If the Norsemen haven't come

I've never seen this house before
and who the hell are you?
Is this something called jamais vu?
I think I'm going to like it,
it actually feels like déja vu.

Yes, I remember this feeling
looking out on Great South Bay
for glinting shields and dragon heads
among all those unmade beds
and children's wounds.

This feels like boarding school,
so of course you can't be trusted,
but I'll make allowances for you
because you're new but not as new
as me. Do you know who I am?

Check your chart while I dress.
We'll pretend we know who we are,
you and I, and by this evening,
if the Norsemen haven't come,
we'll sing hymns in the study hall.

Barbara Brittain

Barbara Brittain in the quince-wry air
touched me dreamily as we passed
or else I would have been a potato
or a twisted puppet in the attic.
That's how it was at boarding school,
some of us keeping others alive,
most of us barely alive ourselves.

I heard her speak to others
but she never said a word to me
and it wouldn't have meant as much
as the savor in her fingertips.
She should be at my funeral
or I should be at hers,
but we don't know each other.

In this way our lives aren't what they seem to be
owing as much as they do to memory.
It's because of Barbara Brittain I believe
in angels and all the possibilities
I don't resent for never coming to me.
It's because of her I never gave up
thinking my home was just a touch away.

Homesick

I want to go home
I've always wanted to go home
do you know where home is

> What if I knew
> what if I'd known

Here is never where it should be
when you want to go home
there is unimaginable

That twitch on the tip of the tongue
that sense of something impending
the floor and the stairs slipping away

> semblance & chimera
> pass for home

Leaving boarding school

Blackberry fort and privet chapel,
did they shudder the moment I left
with my yellow cardboard suitcase,
did Skippy with her crazy eyes,
Dolly and Daisy in their fedoras?
I think two plow horses and a collie
would notice more than people
since they had nothing to hide.

I had forgotten these details,
black taxi, the Messerschmidt 109
that German POWs made for me,
so I assume the loop in my head
that lands me in that driveway
on that particular day portends
some counterclockwise closure
that may enable me to forgive

even if I can't remember names,
enable me to forgive their scents
and above all their silences
because as surely as I go back
that hemp burns their necks too—
they know that almost lynching me
makes lovers' eyes an inquisition
and each honor a bloody throat.

You saw nothing?

The corpse

Worry concrete block and rope,
worry their burden, currents;
it has a story to tell, a memory
that needs to rise to light.

The rope remains nostalgic
for the murk, the memory lies
on the dock a sodden rebuke
to my cunning public story.

But something must be done
now the subject is brought up:
the trouble with getting old
is how new old memories become,

tearing up faces lies have worn
until I consent to take the job
of being what I might have been
were it not so important to please.

I think each of us must be reborn
before we die or wallow in cliché,
so let the corpse come up to say
how it was murdered in its youth.

The source

Coffee and blood are easier to scrub
than a sob instilled in the crib
and I doubt beetles and flies
will put an end to its work.

Sorrow's a word compared to a sob,
which is a thing, a revenant
assigned to the body's rooms
to try doors and sound planks.

If evildoers understood
they would bid for it at auction
and think gold and diamonds algebraic signs
of its remorseless intent to harm.

Who put it there now hides in death.
I will forgive but not forget
because whatever I have to say
rises in that deep, cold wrong.

Portent

Craze of lightning mimes
a Border Collie's eyes:
world unbearably alert
to alien appearances.

This is the light of intent;
what moves in it ignores
your comforts. Remember
as much detail as you can.

Your life depends on it
because when the storm has passed
its creatures have just begun
to perform tests on you.

You saw nothing? In that case
your first test was your last:
ignore the occasional chimera
and otherlings in certain eyes.

Zero messages

I'm not message material,
crackling with threat as I am
of saying something
nobody wants to hear,
especially you, you know
who you are, the one
who exerts every effort
not to hear that one thing
I'm most liable to say.
I think my blue caul
forespoke this curse
of looking about to say
that one dread thing,
whatever it happens to be
at the moment. And yet
my voicemail's silence
belies my life in the street
where people lean to me
wondering why.

If I am dragged by the feet

to a place that no longer exists
where a giant bear lurks in an attic
that reeks of mothballed peril
I will sniff old nemeses in my bed
gathering their sexual heat and fetor
for the one encounter I have shirked
in a junkyard of excuses

A better view

To part the darkness with my hands
reminds me of a wizardry
and conviction once familiar
and now lost. A child is clinging
to my coat, my coat is feathering
the ground, the ground is rising
to provide a better view
of my next great task,
and although I see it clearly
I can't remember what to do,
but that I have the power to do it
I have no doubt, and it is not a dream.

Divine zanies

Zanies unallowed,
flame too flickery;
no one unalloyed
by mock gravitas
& high commerce
may volunteer
for this death march.

Children must be divine
for history to be about them
or fearsomely unwanted
& yet it is utterly about
our destruction of them,
so threatening
is their innocence.

The sob

Who offers this catch in my breath
I gratefully accept   this stifled gasp
I disguise as sob?   What perfect horror
entertained me   at the implant
of companionable sorrow   inoculating me
against vulgar joy   and accepting
that things are what they seem to be?

Look, look over there, we say to a child
as we steal his trust   and leave instead
this sore spot   in his heart if
he's sentimental   or his lung if
he can never breathe   deeply enough
to decipher love   or even pheromones.
Do you remember who told you to look away?

Confession

I've never wanted anything as much
as my Jack Armstrong tiger's eye ring
but I've been very good at faking it.

With the help of British movies
I've chosen what I ought to want
and properly despaired of getting it.

But the ring arrived on time.
As promised, it shone in the dark.
I didn't know nothing else ever would.

Well, I guess that's not exactly true—
I cast a kind of Luminol that tells
where people's thoughts have been.

Yeah, yeah, I know it's magic thinking,
but thoughts leave prints and scents
and even throw intent ahead.

My reward for eating my Wheaties
was better than my reward for growing up
and I'm still pigging out on hope.

Afterward

What was it but a rolling fit,
an aftershock and fugue?
The boy tires who games adults,
his mimicry of life subsides,
his blood crawls deeper
into his core of mistrust.
Withal, he knows what it was about,
to follow the lights in the marsh
and to come back illumined
if only in a spectral flash
that, emboldened, he calls a life.

Viruses and mites

I prefer viruses and mites
to memories corrupting
the dailiness of life.

True catastrophe ripples
from a pinhole in the retina
of time, the rest is just event.

News-stream and hoopla dull
us to the tragedy of children
we leave in attic boxes.

We post celebrities to guard
victims hidden from public view
while we party on news.

A stain that spreads for sixty years
I wore around and called batik.
It's more vivid now than when

it was a drop of blood in bed
and I trembled fearing morning
would or wouldn't come.

Catastrophe

This morning we are stranger than yesterday
and will be too familiar by tonight.
The vigilant suffer this divine disease
with the forbearance of godlings
until they tire of appearances
and pick up the note dropped
at the moment of catastrophe
when everything becomes too loud
too bright too near too large
and must be given names
to disguise the track.

Crystal ship

Doppelganger employment agency

Toward the end of my life I woke up
(how toward I may never be able to say)
to jot a few notes for such fellow revenants
as may wish to consider where they have been.

I wonder what he did with his life,
the boy I left back there to live it.

How did he navigate the egoists
and bring lightning to ground?

I use his missing pieces in these poems
wondering what he did with parts of me
through which storms blew, seas rushed
and people passed so regularly
and so used me with their fingers
I hardly caught their names.

Where was I and am I now,
certainly no friend to that poor boy?

I hope his antigens fought off the retinues
of eyes sharp for alien traits and women eager
to take offense. I hope his remaining parts—
grafts of correct emotion, transplants
of an admired demeanor—cooperated
with his head stuck in the door while my feet
ran barefoot over shards so as not to be heard
by the night watchman in the library
nobody but the authorized may use.

He was more willing to produce his papers
than this scarecrow, this anarchic gholem.

I am a doctoral sleepwalker. My research
is insured against awakening.
I left him sleeping under a bench
in a lightly falling snow. I kissed
his forehead boozily and walked uptown
convinced he would do a better job as me
than I would have done for both of us.

I can't blink for summoning night
or ghosting up a foggy river
mistaking taillights for red buoys,
dodging tankers up to their plimsolls in dread.
I hope this isn't how it is with him.

I left him with the gift of not being me.
It wasn't much but wisely invested
I thought he might end up in Taormina
publishing poems privately
like Cavafy entertaining friends.

No. I hadn't wit or kindness then
to wish him such a lovely thing.
If I had I would have stayed.

I don't think he joined the Foreign Legion
as the dean at Columbia suggested
or became a sandhog or a bartender;
I think he ran a doppelganger employment agency
and disappeared while having his feet massaged
in a warm rain in a stone garden.

The pleasure of my absence

what is as refreshing as the thought of the absence of this mook
spending so much time landscaping and weeding his grievances?
not only can his dwindling hours now be refreshed but also those
who accepted invitations to his exhibitionism. praise this justice;
nothing is belated. he packs up this new state of grace with care
but worries that he will not remember it when he arrives: where?
what is more reassuring than ash poured upon the wind? imagine
how remindful a boor can be, squalid ego sitting on a mountain
saying fond farewell to winged id, this mook set free to become
almost anything else. how better to spend last hours than to think
of one's absence noticed as much as I noticed love and other gifts?
not just dessert but recollection, a time to savor what is disdained.
we should write our own eulogies, then incinerate them with us,
an exercise for the job of remembering where we have been.
my neighborhood already glistens with my absence, trees prepare
for an exuberant shrug and flowers thrill to signals from the stars.

Sounds of corduroy

He turns to heron form
before my eye can fix on him
to live in dusks of mirrors
—changeable country,
variable geometry—
going to and fro,
walking up and down
trackless in the snow.
He pulls in his shadow,
soaks up the light.
His journey ear to ear
fills my brain at night
with sounds of corduroy.
I don't know who he is,
what he bodes, but
it does not promise dawn.

Calliope

I see him close-hauled headed north
the moon haunting his turquoise sails
and I know his mind better than mine
because he is going somewhere for me

not as much surrogate as projection
the navigator I am when I disappear
looking at you as coolly as a hawk
the sailor whose black-hulled boat

casts no shadows on icebergs
and leaves no wake among floes—
I am the shadow that needs no light
having taken light to myself

Don't know about his passage-making
didn't when we were one but I notice
the transom of Calliope bears no homeport
which is as divine as amnesia gets

If I were an aspen

If I were an aspen my jagged rings
would hint at evil stories,
but you wouldn't know this unless
you cut me down, a sacrilege:
faces are forensic enough
if we look past what we want to see
to where there's no way home.
I wish you no chainsaw accidents,
no crushing events, only
nostalgia for a shimmering leaf
neither of us now may hold.

Blue corn

Why don't the clerks let me in,
didn't I follow him here?
Ratty coat, pinched hat,

he's playing with toy cars
behind the steamy windows,
the one who put his arm around me

in the street, whom I embraced,
and if this is Eighth Avenue
in the fifties why am I batiked blue

from crashing through wet cornfields?
I'm drawn to this amiable dream
and eager to see it through

but the toilet calls, bum knees
and the grand compulsion to finish
what I began should I remember it.

Meanwhile I think I'll spend today
savoring why the subject of my nostalgia
would close a shop in my face.

Memory radioactive

Memories are enriched uranium—
there will be accidents and deaths
because they cannot be contained;
it's not exactly picking up sticks
to move these rods around
and finally what kills us
is what leaks into adventures.
                    Memory radioactive
burns holes in tomorrows
that cannot be sealed by hope.

Incident report

Few of us scrub out
or have the courtesy not to stain
rentals with our excrescence
but I think the breed exists
that takes its crime scenes with it
and is invisible to Luminol.

We are the legatees of what?
Our light wands see it
but can't describe its color
or assign it worth.
Is this the scent of Mignonette
drying in a drawer?

These things I came upon,
were they meant for me to see
or must I live another life
to learn not to lift the hem,
the merriment exposed
by careful accident?

Years deciduous

If the bitters of my mind,
specters too raw to croak,
were hung on trees their light
would blind owls and grant
the safety of scurrying things,
gash the fetid beasts
that crash about the woods
and part the reeds of bogs.
Morning would never come,
Leonids would brand
the steamy hide of earth
and my years deciduous
would bathe in sweat
and sail my blood to sea.

Request reassignment

My work as their underthings
in spite of its success as disguise
is drowning me in sorrow
so innocent are their secrets,
inexplicable their shame.

I fear I'm getting hooked
on the scents and lovely silliness
of their desires. It's hard
not to intervene, to be still
and yet anointed in their pain.

I'm dowdy or too skimpy
or give too little support,
I fondle, listen and absorb:
six months of their nakedness
is more than a spy can bear.

I can't explain the seizures
they attribute to another's charm
even though I've had ample time
on cold floors, in rude company
and in hot water to consider it.

They call it love but they're adept
at euphemism and evasion.
Still, I haven't ruled it out
as a rogue element unique
to this illusory place.

I'd like a new posting,
less rub, more dispassion,
a vacation from intimacy,
a chance to rest in motion,
something like a thunderclap.

The crystal ship

A rose awakens at night to home
on werewolves and crystal ships,
a rose resembling certain smiles
that deform the face or glitter
like shattered glass, a rose
that folds upon an ancient moment
too feral for these fawning times.

In rare cases death may occur
when these smiles favor you,
and while roses won't kill you
they will give you that one look
that keeps all you want away.
If any of this makes sense to you
you were born downwind of trouble.

Blood and all that

Your birthday

Enough about you,
    Love, Mom.

Don't try to tell your story,
don't trade secrets away;
you're going to need it
to generate light.

What they didn't want to hear,
Mom and the other delusionals,
you need that to get there from here.

Don't let them tinker
or redact.
Your story's not an heirloom.
You can spin it all by yourself,
but only you know where you hid
the truth, your ticket
to the crystal ship
nobody will ever see but you.

Lots of luck with this project,
your amazing grace;
the rest is a birthday card.

Elegy

My job, to remind you of a savage hurt,
could not have been easier had I been blind.
Wherever I stumbled I touched a sore
concealer hid from lovers and friends
but not from this fiend of your womb.
A job done best is done unawares;
how else could I live up to expectations?

Medusa

What's making you sad
is this and that and the other thing, you say,
the other thing being that glance
that keeps on trying to turn you to stone,
remorseless as an eagle.

What is there but sad
for us cursed paranoids?
Lovelies and bozos though we are,
born to catch that stare,
the rest of it's a stumble
none of our acts sort out.

Whose mother is Medusa?
The boy who looks as if he's going to say
the thing she's dying not to hear?
The boy who looks as if he sees too much
is the one who catches that stare,
that death of cold and sentence
to crumble as he walks away.

Sepia

Who should have these photographs
    so unimportant to heirs,
      tensions time and death ignore?

Sepia angels unable to lift themselves
    from gravity of discovery here,
      who are we if angels are misplaced?

Where are we that it takes photographs
    to see what we spend lives denying?
      What qualifies me as archivist

of a world to which my birth was no visa?
    How did this enemy combatant
      come by such intelligence?

I note the disposition of these bodies:
    my mother in her Saturnian hat,
      lovers revolving around her.

I must have been a fireball, a kind of gnat
    to this planetary system, incinerating
      beyond society's concern or sight.

No prophylactic or lead suit can protect me
    from the study of memorabilia;
      my tears will drown me first.

Something's wrong with you, my mother said.
    I'm sure that Nazi eugenicists
      were equally as persuasive,

so what to do with these fey algorithms
   which I've run out of time to use
   unless of course I can take them with me?

Followers

A dead child often pulls
parents into its grave;
rebuff is like that
erasing life imagined
after loss large as mothers.

It's easier to mourn the dead
than those who shut a door;
in any case, we are most likely
to catch a death of cold
crossing that killing field.

Neither idyll nor idol

Outgrowing earth is the easy part,
it's figuring out what to do
when we're no longer children
that astounds us, where to go,
making the proper calculations
for filing out of these illusions:
we've seen fey children become
sly children, each generation,
and we see none of us was meant
to be an idol and that the end
is recognition: there is no end
but endless growing up.

all two want

where she died
a door's ajar
to follow through
a passage sealed
the janitor marks
& in a thousand years
when all is gone
it will still be there
& when I am gone
someone else will see it
& disappear
leaving a facsimile

that someone
is the one I look for
to take this message
saying wait for me
I am juggling crises
too importantly
but I will tire & then
we will be all
two ever want to be

Blood and all that

She liked me better when I was this
or that, but never at the moment,
liked me better getting off the floor
and stumbling out the door, better
when I claim to be all right, least
when in danger of winning anything,
someone or something like a life.

I like her face better in repose,
not smiling for effect, unhappy
to see me a day out of loserdom.
No joy upsetting her applecart,
its polished rotten Red Delicious
looking so much like family values
and all our deadly pharmaceuticals.

Sorry, dear, for a little honesty,
perhaps a small success, and sorrier
for life spent on misunderstanding.
No, dear, I didn't go out and get a life,
I got a moment's clarity and decided
to send a little murderous bubble
into one of those celebrated blood ties.

Tree of lies

Ominous gurgling

I will suspend tomorrow at 4 a.m.
to think about the alternatives
(they make good bookmarks).
A sunrise without a future
even a modest 20-hour one
is a sobering event considering
most days are just another drink.

You may not think I can do this,
that I don't know enough about time,
but I know what is truly fabulous
is our power to suspend anything
that requires a little examination,
so don't cross any threshholds
if you wake up at 4 a.m.

or you'll end up a tourist
in that netherworld toilets portend,
the one you started to suspect
the first time you hid in a closet.
Certainties mislead but cracks
and ominous gurglings suggest
splendor is unauthorized.

A bargain basement

Even angels have their price.
I would have settled for Wonder Woman
or a knock-off of her bracelet,
but this guy wanted my name.
Can you imagine that, my good name?
What a bogus protest I put up!
My name for protection, what a deal!
What the hell did I need it for?
Nobody could pronounce or spell it.
What did I need any name for?
I'd just be me and he'd be this angel-mook
with a borrowed name,
                              so who got raped?
We'd talk about it again in fifty years
after drunkenness and sobriety
and other near-death experiences.
Now let's talk about it to hell and gone,
talk about angels with terrorists' names,
talk about how your face comes off
with masks until you can't remember
your face when you gave up your name
to have a friend in this friendless place.

On having casual gods

I wore out my welcome in the womb,
my worth was in being put behind.
I was told milk made me vomit
but who feeds a baby fire and blood?
Everyone goes back to Waukegan
or Nu Yawk; this bedroom has no floor.
Plumbing works better somewhere else—
endearing words have bad breath.
I feared you'd go away before I met you;
how could you see me through that?
You hadn't winked the Internet to life;
you were swigging in the kitchen with Ma Bell,
and I knew if you gave me 100 more years
I'd still be gagging on milk and acting smarmy
just so you wouldn't look over my shoulder.
I'm going to rest and let a cataclysm
press me into a precious jewel.

Dragon croquet

If you were to tell me I am God
I would take it calmly having been
told other outlandish things

and believed more than is good for a man
a man I say because you haven't told me yet
that I am God but I expect you to

because all there is left to do
is cooperatively manage this mess
because I shouldn't have to say

I made a hash of it all by myself
and you shouldn't have to confess
you need all us little godlings

taking sweet history to hatch
while laughing dragons bat us
through burning hoops with their tails

Being kicked to death

I collected the big pimp's cut
      from hat check hookers
in twenty dives. I wore
      youth and college looks
to hide the work from cops
      and fellow scum.
I watered orange juice
      in theater concessions,
muled heroin on subways,
      delivered every bag and g.
I know about heroism—
      goes with great legs and despair,
and I can tell you how it feels
      to get kicked to death
for dumping a bag of H
      I was supposed to hold
and getting rescued
      by Vinny from Staten Island,
my stepfather's goombah.
      I don't have the cartilage
to anchor my ribs
      and I still don't breathe right,
so I remember these things
      as if I were in Saint Vincent's
listening to the mafiosi
      telling the intern why
I had to be treated
      as if I mattered. He got worse,

that pimp with the big feet,
    he lost his empire
for beating a little schmuck
    with interesting connections.

A death on West End Avenue

I drew D in my steamy blood on the curb,
then I staggered home and showered.
The cabbie was killing me until I got his balls;
I'd puked in his nice clean cab at 4 a.m.,
but that's not the story, the story is D,
which for a long time I thought was me,
an eon of falling down behind my eyes
until infirm and white I remembered them,
me and Dolores, young magi
pouring hope into play tea cups,
never dreaming anyone meant goodbye.
Only the electric moment was forever
and that is all that tidal D recalled.

Stoic's instruction

Don't call anybody with word of my death,
don't interfere with the work of leaf fall
or any of the sacred things I've loved.

Down with all triumphals and celebrations
announcing us as somehow grander
than what is going on around us.

A hawk will stoop, a twig set sail,
and that will suffice to mark my passage;
more than that is hubris, even my saying so.

Tree of lies

Tonight I drape my lies on yew
to cavort in a quarry pool
with snakes and Leonids—
may naked faeries lift
my lies for underthings
and blow me kisses as I rise,
ball lightning, to mountain tops,
peak to peak across the world,
free of what I've said,
delighted to be dead.

Coda

Magic act

You walk away, I follow,
you turn around, it's not you.
I have to take back what I said,
whatever it was. It's-not-you
is gone and someone yanks me
out of the way of a cab
and I'm back on the curb
waiting for the light to change
so I can go to I don't know where
just in time to be there
at the right moment to recognize
you not expecting me
to loom up in front of you.
Look up from the pigeon shit
on my shoes to the face I wore
that day in the salt fen
when we knew we'd never come back.
We're still there no matter
how many times we repeat this act,
even if I get run over
and you don't turn around.